Gospel and Law

BAMPTON LECTURES IN AMERICA
NUMBER 3
DELIVERED AT COLUMBIA UNIVERSITY

1950

Gospel and Law

THE RELATION OF FAITH AND ETHICS
IN EARLY CHRISTIANITY

By C. H. DODD

PROFESSOR EMERITUS IN THE UNIVERSITY

OF CAMBRIDGE, ENGLAND

CAMBRIDGE
AT THE UNIVERSITY PRESS
MCMLI

Published in the United States by Columbia University Press, New York

First printing June, 1951
Second printing December, 1951
Third printing 1952

Printed in the United States of America

Preface

THE LECTURES are here reproduced virtually as they were delivered, with a minimum of revision, but occasionally passages have been included which were omitted in delivery for lack of time. In Chapter IV a few paragraphs have been reproduced, with some modifications, from my Ainslie Memorial Lecture, *The Gospel and the Law of Christ,* with the consent of the publishers, Messrs. Longmans, Green & Co.

C. H. DODD

NEW YORK
JUNE, 1950

Contents

Gospel and Law

1 · Preaching and Teaching in the Early Church

AMONG the religions of the world there are, I suppose, few which have no ethical content at all. Religions which we regard as primitive sometimes surprise us by the comparative elevation of the moral ideas which they contain. At the same time, there are religions, and some of them among the "higher" religions, which so emphasize the mystical, or it may be the ritual, aspect of religion (to use imprecise but serviceable terms) that social ethics seem hardly to count. On the other hand, there are systems of ethics, and some of them very fine and idealistic systems, which either repudiate religion, or, like Confucianism, treat it with a distant and somewhat ironical respect.

The Christian religion, like Judaism (to take another example), is an ethical religion in the specific sense that it recognizes no ultimate separation between the service of God and social behavior. "Thou shalt love the Lord thy God"; "Thou shalt love thy neighbor as thyself." The two basic commandments stand together.

But to say this is not to have resolved the tension which appears always to be latent between religion and ethics. In various contemporary ways of presenting Christianity there are marked divergencies upon this point, as indeed there have been at most periods of its history. In some quarters the strongest emphasis is laid upon the specifically religious elements, by which I mean such things as faith, worship, sacraments, communion with God, the way of salvation, and the hope of eternal life. In other quarters it is the specifically ethical aspect which commands almost exclusive attention—conduct, moral judgments, philanthropy, the Christian social order, and the like. The advocates of the respective views are often severe with one another. Words harmless enough in themselves, such as "mysticism" and "moralism," are hurled about as if they were terms of opprobrium.

It is easy enough to say that both aspects are essential to Christianity and that both are important; even, perhaps, that both are of equal importance and that all that is required is a sound balance. That is true, but it does not go to the root of the matter. It is impossible to understand either the ethical content of Christianity or its religious content unless we can in some measure hold the two together and understand them in their true, organic relations within a whole. This calls for deeper soundings.

In the course of its development through the centuries and its extension to various peoples and cultures, Christianity has acquired an immensely complicated history and a bewildering variety of forms; but it possesses a body of classical documents, the New Testament, which, fortunately, are acknowledged as such by the consent of all branches of the Christian Church; and these documents put us in a position to see what Christianity was like in its beginnings and what were the thoughts and principles by which it was shaped.

We must therefore undertake some examination of the data provided by the New Testament upon the problem before us. We shall approach these in a spirit of historical in-

*But not
with identical
doctrinal
interpretation*

*Religious
v
Ethical*

vestigation, seeking in the first place to recover a picture of the thought and activity of the Christian community in its earliest days, and then proceeding to interpret that picture.

We may begin our survey of early Christian literature with the Pauline Epistles, which, taken as a whole, are the earliest group of documents. Some of these have the character of occasional letters, spontaneous and without any plan or design; but some of them show a definite pattern. They are divided into two main parts. The first part deals with specifically religious themes—deals with them, in the main, in the reflective manner which constitutes theology—and the second part consists mainly of ethical precepts and admonitions. Thus, the twofold character of Christianity as ethical religion is reflected in the very structure of these documents. The second or ethical part is linked organically with the first part, and this link we shall have to examine more closely later on; but the division between the two parts, though it is not absolute, is pretty well marked.

The pattern is clear in the Epistles to the Romans, Galatians, Colossians, and Ephesians, and when it has been recognized in these clear examples, it can be traced by analogy in other epistles, where it is not so obvious at first sight; not only in epistles written by Paul but in those written by other authors as well.

This is hardly accidental. We recognize here a set pattern of composition followed by early Christian writers, corresponding to the structure of their thought. They are presenting Christianity as an ethical religion in which ethics are directly related to a certain set of convictions about God, man, and the world, a set of convictions religious in their subject matter and theological in their expression.

Turn now from the epistles to the gospels. The Gospel according to Matthew, the first in canonical order, contains a large amount of ethical teaching with a certain general similarity to that which we have observed in the epistles, though with some marked differences, to which we shall have to give attention later. This teaching occurs for the most part in fairly large, continuous blocks. The most important and typical of these is the so-called Sermon on the Mount, which occupies three long chapters in succession (chaps. 5–7). It is not, of course, a sermon at all. It is a highly articulated and systematic presentation of the main features of the Christian ethical system. These solid blocks of ethical teaching correspond in some sort to the ethical sections of the epistles. They are inserted into a framework which takes the form of a narrative of events.

When this structure has been recognized in the first gospel, it can be traced also in the second and third. Here, indeed, it is less formal, and story and teaching alternate more freely; yet even so each of these works provides examples of sequences of ethical precepts, more or less complete in themselves, and comparable with those which we found in the epistles; and these are related to passages of narrative which serve to introduce them.

There is therefore in the gospels a duality of structure corresponding to that which we recognized in the epistles. The ethical materials in gospels and epistles alike have a general similarity of form and content, but in the epistles they are related to theological doctrine, while in the

gospels they are related to a narrative of events. The difference, however, is not by any means so great as it seems at
first sight. The narrative and the theology belong together.

vide design¹
¶ each Epstl.

Careful inspection shows that the theological disserta-
tions of the epistles often have imbedded in them fragments
of narrative. When, for example, Paul sets out to discuss
such abstruse doctrines of theology as those of predestina-
tion, election, and justification by faith, in the middle chapters of the Epistle to the Romans (chaps. 9–11), he relates
his discussion throughout to a kind of skeleton outline of
the history of Israel. When he embarks upon the difficult
problem of life after death in the fifteenth chapter of the
First Epistle to the Corinthians, he expressly grounds what
he has to say upon certain historical facts about Jesus Christ
which he says were communicated to him by persons who
were in a position to know.

Let us take a different author. In the Epistle to the
Hebrews, where the author is attempting to define or char-
acterize the profoundly religious ideas of priesthood and
sacrifice and to show in what sense the work of Christ
can be understood in terms of those ideas, he introduces
a strangely vivid and moving reference to the narrative
of Jesus in the Garden of Gethsemane, which is familiar
to us from the gospels (Hebrews 5:7–10).

Perhaps these examples will suffice to justify the conclusion that the theological sections of the epistles are not
without a certain basis in the narrative of events. On the
other hand, the narrative of the gospels, as all recent criticism agrees, is coloured throughout by a religious, if not
a theological, valuation of the events which it records and
of the central Figure in them. The gospels record actual

occurrences, but they record them in a way which betrays their authors' sense of a pervading significance going beyond the mere occurrence. They relate it all through to ideas which are specifically religious and necessarily call for a theological interpretation; such ideas as the kingdom of God and the salvation of mankind.

It turns out, then, that the theology of the epistles and the narrative of the gospels have a motive in common. The writers of the gospels believed that the facts of the career of Jesus Christ were worth recording because they had decisive religious significance which challenged theological interpretation; and the writers of the epistles, presupposing a knowledge of the facts, undertook to explain their significance, and so created Christian theology. It is this inseparable interconnection of religion and theology with historical fact that justifies the description of Christianity as a historical religion; and this is a part of its distinctive genius.

To sum up, the ethical teaching of the New Testament is embedded in a context which consists of a report of historical facts and an explanation of their religious significance, and this fact gives to Christian Ethics a peculiar character, which I shall presently attempt to describe. But before going on to a consideration of the ethical teaching itself, it is necessary to say something about this context in which it is embedded and which has both a historical and a religious aspect in indivisible unity.

According to the evidence of the New Testament, the earliest exponents of the Christian religion worked out a distinctive way of presenting the fundamental convictions of their faith, in a formula which they called "the proclamation." The Greek word here is *kerygma*. Our translators of the Bible commonly render it "preaching"; but in its current implications at the present day the word is misleading. *Kerygma* properly means a public announcement or declaration, whether by a town crier, or by an auctioneer commending his goods to the public, or by the herald of a sovereign state dispatched on a solemn mission, to present an ultimatum, it may be, or to announce terms of peace.

The Christian "preacher" thought of himself as an announcer of very important news. He called it quite simply "the good news," or in our traditional translation, "the gospel." It was this "good news" that was embedded in the "proclamation," the *kerygma*. It was essentially a public announcement of events of public importance.

The form and content of the proclamation, the *kerygma,* can be recovered from the New Testament with reasonable accuracy. It recounted in brief the life and work of Jesus Christ, His conflicts, sufferings, and death, and His resurrection from the dead; and it went on to declare that in these events the divinely guided history of Israel through long centuries had reached its climax. God Himself had acted decisively in this way to inaugurate His kingdom upon earth. This was the core of all early Christian preaching, however it might be elaborated, illustrated, and explained.[1]

The preacher's aim was to convince his hearers that they were, indeed, confronted by the eternal God in His kingdom, power, and glory; that they, like all men, stood under His judgment upon what they had done and upon what

[1] See C. H. Dodd, *The Apostolic Preaching and Its Developments,* London, 1936.

they were, and that this judgment was now immediate and inescapable; further, that those who would put themselves under God's judgment would, through His mercy, find an opportunity open to them to enter upon a new life; that actually, as a result of these facts which they proclaimed, a new era in the relations between God and man had begun.

Those who responded to this appeal and placed themselves under the judgment and mercy of God as declared in Jesus Christ, became members of the community, the Church, within which the new life could be lived. These members were then instructed in the ethical principles and obligations of the Christian life. This course of instruction in morals, as distinct from the proclamation of the gospel, is covered by the term "teaching," which in Greek is *didaché.*

This order of approach, first the proclamation, then the beginning of instruction in morals, first *kerygma,* then *didaché,* seems to have been thoroughly characteristic of the Christian mission; it is precisely this order, first *kerygma,* then *didaché,* which we have seen to be general in the New Testament writings.

This way of approach to ethics was sharply distinguished from that of contemporary Greek moralists, who from the time of Aristotle had set out to provide a self-contained and self-justifying system of ethics. For Christianity, ethics are not self-contained or self-justifying; they arise out of a response to the Gospel.

On the other hand, while the Christian way of approach contrasts with that of Greek moralists, it has a real analogy with the Jewish tradition out of which Christianity arose.

The classical formulation of the moral law in the Old Testament begins, "I am the Lord thy God, which brought thee out of the land of Egypt, out of the house of bondage. Thou shalt have none other gods before me." Then it goes on to lay down such concrete moral precepts as "Thou shalt not kill"; "Thou shalt not commit adultery"; "Thou shalt not steal." That is to say, it begins with a declaration of historical facts religiously understood. The facts were that Israel had escaped out of bondage in the land of Egypt and become a free nation. These facts were understood religiously as meaning that God Himself had intervened to liberate His people. The "commandments" are a corollary to the facts.

Again, if instead of the Decalogue, which is the shortest possible summary of the moral law in the Old Testament, we examine the grand structure of the Torah or Law of Moses (contained in the Pentateuch, or Five Books of Moses), we discern the same character. The extremely concrete and detailed system of regulations is embedded in a narrative of events, which are presented in the guise of "mighty acts of the Lord"; that is to say, they are historical events understood as religiously significant. It is this background, the mighty acts of God, that gives cogency to the commandments of the Torah, for these acts of God established what is described as the "covenant," by which is meant a special relation between this particular people and the God who had delivered them.

Later Judaism distinguished between *haggada,* the declaration or exposition of religious truth, often in the form of a story, and *halakha,* regulations for conduct. This distinction is analogous to the primitive Christian distinction between *kerygma* and *didaché,* the proclamation of the fundamental facts of the Gospel in their religious significance, and moral instruction grounded upon them. In Christianity, as in Judaism, the *kerygma* announces the mighty acts in which God established His new covenant with His people, and the moral obligations set forth in the *didaché* arise within that covenant.

It appears, then, that the problem that we have set ourselves, the problem of the way in which ethics and religion are related in the ethical religion which is Christianity, may be attacked by way of examining the literary records of *kerygma* and *didaché,* the proclamation and the ethical instruction, respectively, and trying to trace the relation between them.

We shall start at the ethical end, by investigating the form and content of ethical instruction in the early church, on the basis of the ethical portions of the epistles. In doing so we shall bear in mind that such instruction, both in the literature and in the established practice of the primitive church, was made to depend upon the affirmations of the *kerygma.*

It appears that the earliest extant Christian writing is Paul's First Epistle to the Thessalonians.[2] As it happens, it provides a useful starting point for our present study. This letter was written by the apostle in the year 50 A. D. to a congregation of newly converted Christians in the city

---

[2] Some critics would place Galatians earlier than I Thessalonians, but the balance of probability seems to me to lean it the other way. It matters little for our purpose. In any case the actual date of I Thessalonians is not in doubt, within a few months, while the date of Galatians remains uncertain.

now called Salonica, in Macedonia. While preaching there he had fallen into trouble with the police and was banished from the city and forbidden to return. He felt some natural anxiety that these new Christians, many of whom had been brought out of paganism only a few weeks before and had had little teaching, should appreciate the moral demands of their new faith. Accordingly, he writes to them as follows (I abridge slightly what he says, but only slightly):

We beg you, we appeal to you, in the Lord Jesus, to be even more diligent than you are, in following the tradition we passed on to you, about the way to please God by your conduct. You know what orders we gave you, by the help of Jesus Christ: it is the will of God that you should be holy, that you should abstain from sexual immorality and learn, each of you, to keep his body in holiness and honor . . . not to overreach his fellow-Christian or to invade his rights. . . . About family affection [within the Christian "family," the Church, he means] it is not necessary for me to write to you. You have God's own teaching, to love one another. [He is referring to the Old Testament commandment, "Thou shalt love thy neighbor as thyself," as re-affirmed by Jesus Christ] and you are in fact practising this rule of love towards all your fellow-Christians in Macedonia. We appeal to you to make even greater efforts. We want you to strive hard to keep calm, to mind your own business, and to work with your hands, as we ordered, so that you may both make a good impression on outsiders and also find your own (economic) needs supplied. (I Thessalonians 4:1-12)

There are several points here that should be observed before we pass on. First, there is the downright peremptory tone which Paul adopts. He neither argues nor offers tactful advice. He gives "orders"; the term which he employs is the term used for army orders. This may come as something of a shock to those who have been accustomed to think of Paul as the apostle of liberty, and even of what is nowadays called "Christian anarchism."

Secondly, the orders are severely practical and commonsense. The Christians of Thessalonica are to observe decent self-control in sexual relations, to respect the rights of others, to do their best to love their neighbors, and to be honest and industrious, so as to maintain a reasonable standard of living without having to keep appealing for charity (like some Christian communities which Paul knew too well). Paul's teaching, then, has its feet well on the ground.

Thirdly, we can hardly be wrong in identifying these "orders" to which the apostle refers, as belonging to the regular course of ethical instruction for converts. The technical term used for it was *catechesis;* hence our word "catechism." That it must have covered a great deal more than is mentioned here, goes without saying. Paul is recalling certain points in this *catechesis* which, he feels, in view of news received from Salonica, need emphasizing. But so far as it goes, this passage gives us trustworthy information of the contents of the Pauline *catechesis*.

As it happens, we can supplement the information we have in this passage from a second letter which the apostle wrote to the same community. We have noticed that one item in the body of instructions was the rule that members of the church should be ready to work with their hands. This salutary rule seems to have been unpopular at Salonica. In the second letter the apostle writes: "When we were with you, we gave orders that if a man was unwilling to work he should not be given food," and he then proceeds to elaborate the point, in view of flagrant refusal to work on the part of some members (II Thessalonians 3:10–12).

Fourthly, in both letters to the Thessalonians Paul speaks of the body of instructions he had given as "traditions." He uses the same term in writing upon matters of conduct to the Corinthians, where he prefaces a fresh piece of teaching with a tactful acknowledgment that the Corinthians have faithfully followed the orders which they had previously been given. "I commend you," he writes, "because you remembered what I said and preserved the traditions which I passed on to you" (I Corinthians 11:2).

Of course, every tradition must be started by someone, and it is arguable that Paul was, in fact, the originator of the "tradition" of ethical teaching to which he refers. In that case, the passages we have noted would tell us about nothing more than Paul's own established practice. But it would be entirely unnatural to understand his words in that sense, especially as in the same letter to the Corinthians he also speaks of a "tradition" regarding the facts about Jesus and expressly says that he had received it from others and handed it on to his correspondents (I Corinthians 15:1–3). We may take it, therefore, that there was already a traditional body of ethical teaching given to converts from paganism to Christianity. Paul could safely assume that such teaching was given in churches outside his own sphere of influence, as appears from a place in his letter to the Christians of Rome, a city which he had not yet visited. He expresses thankfulness that the Roman Christians wholeheartedly obey what he calls "the pattern of teaching" which they had received, proving thereby, he says, that they had been liberated from sin and made into servants of what is right (Romans 6:17–18).

There seems to be evidence here both for the existence of a definite form of ethical instruction or *catechesis* in the earliest days of the Christian mission to the Roman Empire and for some part, at least, of its contents. Our knowledge of any further contents must be derived from the study of passages in the epistles which seem to recall, sometimes directly and sometimes allusively, the well-established pattern of catechetical training through which their readers had been put when they first became Christians. It is a delicate matter to decide in any given case whether we are in fact being referred to such an established pattern, or whether the writer is developing fresh teaching for the occasion.

Thus, in Galatians 5:13 Paul is clearly making a transition from the rather controversial theology of the earlier chapters to ethical instruction. He begins by reminding his correspondents that the whole law can be summed up in the commandment "Thou shalt love thy neighbour as thyself." This is certainly traditional. In the verses that follow, down to the end of chapter v, the case is not so clear. There is a list of vices to be avoided, which recalls similar lists of vices to be found in pagan moralists and their Jewish imitators, and may well have found its way into Christian tradition; with a balancing list of virtues which may already have been traditional in Christian circles, but is, perhaps, more likely to have been compiled by Paul himself. The way in which the whole passage is tied up with the distinctively Pauline doctrine of the

Spirit expounded in the earlier chapters suggests that we have here an *ad hoc* development of traditional material, rather than anything like an extract from it. With 6:1 we perhaps return to something more directly taken from tradition: "If a man is detected in any misbehaviour, you who are spiritual must put him right, very gently, and with great care lest you should be tempted yourselves. Bear one another's burdens, and in this way you will fullfil the law of Christ." The language of the passage is thoroughly Pauline, and we should, perhaps, not have suspected that the matter of it was traditional, but that it clearly alludes to regulations for the treatment of offenders in the church which are to be found in Matthew 18:15–17. It is significant that Paul expressly refers these injunctions to "the law of Christ."

But the soundest method of determining, with the highest degree of probability which the nature of the case admits, the contents of the early Christian "pattern of teaching," as Paul calls it, is to examine the ethical portions of a number of epistles, and see whether the material common to them all betrays any signs of originating at a stage antedating the particular writing. The enterprise is limited by the fact that most of the relevant documents are either by Paul or else were written directly under his influence, so that it is arguable that whatever is common to them attests only Paul's masterful mind. But, in the first place, it is now almost certain that the Epistle to the Hebrews and the First Epistle of Peter contain much more that is independent and original than earlier criticism admitted; and in the second place, even in the Pauline epistles themselves there are some recurrent features of language and style in the ethical sections which seem to set them apart, as if the apostle were not writing entirely freely, in his own natural manner, but following a partly stereotyped pattern.

Anyone who will read the epistles with attention, and pay regard to style and form as well as to content, cannot fail to recognize, even in translation, a common style in certain passages, different from the normal style of the writers concerned. Take as examples the following three short passages, as they stand in the Revised Standard Version.

[I] We exhort you, brethren, admonish the idle, encourage the faint-hearted, help the weak, be patient with them all. See that none of you repays evil for evil, but seek to do good to one another and to all. Rejoice always, pray constantly, give thanks in all circumstances; for this is the will of God in Christ Jesus for you.

[II] Let brotherly love continue. Do not neglect to show hospitality to strangers, for thereby some have entertained angels unawares. Remember those who are in prison, as though in prison with them, and those who are ill-treated, since you also are in the body.

[III] Have unity of spirit, sympathy, love of the brethren, a tender heart and a humble mind. Do not return evil for evil, or reviling for reviling; but on the contrary bless, for to this you have been called, that you may obtain a blessing.

It would, I think, puzzle even a person well read in the New Testament to say, on grounds of style alone, to what authors these extracts are to be assigned. They are so much alike. They are all marked by a concise, staccato style. They use the fewest words possible. They have a kind of sing-song rhythm, which helps the memory.[3] As a matter of fact, the first is by Paul (I Thessalonians 5:14–18), the second from the Epistle to the Hebrews (13:1–3), and the third from the First Epistle of Peter (3:8–9): The author to the Hebrews has a strongly individual style, deeply influenced by Greek rhetoric and entirely different from Paul's, which again is unmistakably individual. The style of the First Epistle of Peter is less individual, yet it is sufficiently distinctive to bring out the difference between such passages as that which I have quoted and the bulk of the epistle.

I do not think it plausible to suggest that all this is accidental; nor would it be any more plausible to suggest that the authors of Hebrews and I Peter said to themselves, "Since Paul changes his style when he comes to ethical teaching, we will do the same." It is surely more likely that each of these writers was unconsciously influenced by the ring and run of familiar forms of ethical instruction in the church. I do not suppose that in such passages we have anything like a direct reproduction of an existing document, or even verbal quotation of an established form transmitted by word of mouth. But it does seem probable on

[3] In Greek, passages of this type show certain peculiarities of grammar and idiom. The most remarkable is the use of a participle where an imperative would be expected. This is entirely unGreek, and appears to be an imitation of a Hebrew idiom which is not infrequent in certain types of Jewish ethical instruction. It is not found in the epistles outside of these characteristic passages of ethical teaching, but in such passages it is employed by Paul in Romans and Colossians, by Paul or an imitator in Ephesians, and by other writers in Hebrews and I Peter. This seems to be conclusive evidence that all are following some common model.

general grounds that we are here indirectly in touch with a common tradition. Different writers develop and elaborate the common pattern at different points and in characteristically different ways, but tend to return to it where they are not concerned to emphasize any particular point.

It appears, then, that the ethical portions of the epistles are based upon an accepted pattern of teaching which goes back to a very early period indeed, and whose general form and content can be determined with considerable probability.

It seems to have run somewhat as follows: The convert is first enjoined to lay aside certain discreditable kinds of conduct, especially some which were common and easily condoned in pagan society. Sometimes lists of such vices are inserted, lists which can be shown to have been drawn from popular ethical teaching of the period, quite outside Christianity. The convert is enjoined to abandon these vices and to be prepared for a total reorientation of moral standards in a Christian sense. This is sometimes expressed in the terms "to put off the old man and to put on the new."

Next, some of the typical virtues of the new way of life are set forth, with especial emphasis upon such virtues as purity and sobriety, gentleness and humility, generosity and a hospitable temper, patience under injuries, and readiness to forgive.

Then various social relationships are reviewed, in particular those which constitute the family as the primary form of community; the relations of husband and wife, parents and children, master and servants—for, in the social structure of the time, a servant, even if he were a slave, was a member of the *familia.* The proper Christian attitude in all such relations is briefly indicated: husbands are to love their wives, children to obey their parents, masters to treat their servants with consideration, and so forth.

Then the wider "family" of the Christian community itself comes into view. The new member is enjoined to respect the leaders or elders of the society and is taught that each member has his own special function in the body, for which he is responsible.

Looking farther afield, he is given some counsel about behavior to his pagan neighbors in the delicate situation in which the members of an unpopular sect were likely to find themselves. He must be prudent, nonprovocative, seeking peace, never flouting the social or moral standards of those among whom he lives, while using any opportunity of doing a kindness to them even if they had not been friendly to him.

Like other subjects of the Empire, he is told, he owes obedience to the constituted authorities and should make it a matter of conscience to keep the law and pay his taxes. But there are limits beyond which a higher allegiance claims him: he must be loyal at all cost to his faith, and prepared to endure persecution with inflexible determination and fortitude.

Finally he is reminded of the extremely critical time in which he lives, which calls for constant watchfulness and lays upon him the most solemn responsibilities.

Such is the general scheme which, with large variations

of detail, reappears so often in these writings that we cannot but conclude that it was part of the common and primitive tradition of the church.[4]

It is filled in and elaborated variously in different writings. We shall later have to take account of this elaboration, because it is there that we may detect some of the ways in which the fundamental convictions of the Gospel make their impact upon ethics; but for the present we recognize in the ethical teaching which is represented by the epistles, a practical scheme for the guidance of organized groups in the Roman Empire faced with the common problems of social behavior, in a situation which in some ways made such problems more difficult for them than for other people.

In the Graeco-Roman world of the first century, the Christian church was not the only agency which aimed at elevating the moral standards of society. Judaism had long been a missionary religion. Hellenistic Judaism in particular had worked out a technique for approach to pagans, mainly on ethical lines. It won many proselytes, and its influence spread far beyond the limits of membership of the synagogue. Hellenistic Jewish missionaries had learned much as regards method from the preachers of popular philosophy, who went from city to city and often found

---

[4] The study of primitive Christian *catechesis* owes much to the work of Philip Carrington (now Archbishop of Quebec) in *The Primitive Christian Catechism* (Cambridge, 1940), and E. G. Selwyn (Dean of Winchester), in an important appendix to his commentary on *The First Epistle of St. Peter* (London, 1946). I am indebted to both, even though I do not necessarily accept the details of their conclusions.

ready audiences. These wandering philosophers mostly put forward some version of the fine, austere moral code of the Stoics, adapted for popular appeal.

We have a fair amount of evidence of the way in which these precursors of the Christian mission, both Jewish and pagan, went about their task. It seems clear that the early Christians were influenced by their example. For instance, known Jewish forms for receiving proselytes show parallels to elements in the Christian *catechesis,* such as the insistence upon a radical reorientation of moral standards, and upon membership in a society carrying solemn obligations; such, again, as the recital of typical commandments which the convert will be expected to observe, and the warning of the danger of persecution, with demands for constancy.

Again, there is the method of setting forth moral obligations under the head of typical social relations: duties of husbands and wives, parents and children, masters and servants, duties to the commonwealth and the government. The passages of the epistles which deal with this theme are similar in style and manner to the popular teaching both of Hellenistic Judaism and of Stoicism. Not infrequently parallels to the actual precepts can be found, and have been set out at length by scholars.

In broad outline, therefore, it appears that the ethical teaching given by the early church was pretty closely related to the general movement in Graeco-Roman society towards the improvement of public morals as it was undertaken in the first century by various agencies. Christian teachers took for granted the existing structure of society, with its known moral problems and dangers. Up to a point, they were able to adopt a good deal of the basic criticism and counsel which serious moralists of other schools were urging on their contemporaries.

They were certainly wise in thus linking up the teaching they gave with the accepted standards of the society in which their converts moved. There is always a certain danger about a movement which aims at making its members superior to the commonly recognized standards. With unstable characters there is always the risk that, once emancipated from the accepted conventions, they will fall below them instead of rising above them, and lapse into eccentricity or worse. It shows therefore, much wisdom in these early Christian teachers that they kept their converts' feet firmly on the ground, by reminding them continually of the accepted fundamental obligations of society. It was extremely healthy (for example) for the Thessalonians to be told, "It is the will of God that you should be honest and industrious"; and for the Romans to be told, "It is the will of God that you should obey the law and pay your taxes"; whatever other and higher demands Christianity might make upon them.

When we have recognized the fact that in general structure the *catechesis* of early Christianity followed the lines of other ethical teaching of the time, we shall be better prepared to recognize the points at which specifically Christian motives and sanctions are introduced. We shall discover within the framework of a workaday code of behavior the impact of ideas which go far to transform the whole moral situation; and this will lead us to appreciate the deeper connections between Christian ethics and the religious springs from which they took their rise.

2 · Principles and Motives of Christian Ethics in the New Testament

THE ethical teaching of the early church, we have seen, falls into a scheme of practical precepts for everyday living, a scheme based upon a realistic recognition of the structure of society as it then was, and following in general outline the patterns of ethical teaching which were being set forth by teachers of other schools. The teaching of the church was thus assured of direct relevance to the situation of those to whom it was addressed.

We have now to recognize within this general pattern certain specific points at which distinctively Christian motives or sanctions appear. I shall mention four such points, and I shall try to show how at these points ethical ideas are transformed by being brought into a context which is religious through and through, being defined by the Gospel itself as it is contained in the *kerygma*.

The four points at which, above all, the Christian ethic in the New Testament betrays such direct dependence upon the Gospel, may be labeled as follows: first, Christian eschatology; secondly, the idea of the "Body of Christ"; thirdly, the imitation of Christ; and fourthly, the primacy of love or charity.

1. *Christian Eschatology.*—If one has been making a stay, mentally, in the Hellenistic world of the first century,

and then comes back to the New Testament, there is nothing in the latter which gives one a greater sense of strangeness than the language which its writers use about the end of the world, the last judgment, the second advent of Christ and similar themes, which are generally comprehended under the term "eschatology." The implication of all such language is that the writers believed themselves to be living in a unique period of the world's history, when portentous events were in process in which they themselves were involved, unprecedented in previous history and leading up to an almost unimaginable climax. This belief was uncongenial to much of the best religious thought of the first century, and it is uncongenial to a great deal of modern thought; but it pervades most of the New Testament in one form or another, and its influence on ethical ideas must have been considerable.

The background of this belief lies in pre-Christian Judaism, which adopted the interpretation of history put forward by the prophets of ancient Israel. This interpretation differed widely from that which was current among Greek-thinking people at the time. In the Hellenistic world, in the main, history was held to move in preordained cycles. For Judaism, history was a movement toward a goal, directed by a purpose. The purpose was the purpose of God, and was animated by the justice and the mercy of God.

The goal of history was presented in imaginative pictures. How else could it possibly be depicted, since it lies beyond all human experience? These imaginative pictures are, to our taste, sometimes quite fantastic. We must do their authors the simple justice of not taking them with the unimaginative literalness which is characteristic of our Western minds. The detail of them, however, need not be considered for our present purpose. In any case, these imaginative pictures of the goal of history imply that at last the full purpose of God would disclose itself in an event which should conclusively express both His justice and His mercy. This event, therefore, would bring upon men at once judgment and salvation, judgment absolute and salvation absolute, and would reveal the Kingdom of God, that is to say, the sovereignty of God over His world.

For some, this great event was the absolute end of history, after which nothing at all would happen. It would be succeeded by some form of existence totally different from anything that we can either experience or imagine. For others, it was the beginning of a new age of history in which the power of God would be signally at work.

Early Christians believed that this event had happened. Consequently, it could now be described not merely in terms of fantasy or imagination, but in part at least in terms of history and experience. The Kingdom of God had been inaugurated on earth in an act which was both God's judgment on the iniquities of men and the supreme opportunity afforded by His mercy for forgiveness and a fresh start. That was the meaning of the coming of Christ, and in particular of His death and resurrection. It was the crucial event of history. Perhaps it was the last event; perhaps it would be immediately completed by the winding up of history in the last judgment; so at least some of them thought. The extent to which that belief prevailed has perhaps been exaggerated, but some early Christians certainly held it. Of course, things did not work out in that way. The world did not come to an end. In view of the facts, the church accepted a revision of its early expectations.

The result of all this was a certain tension which can be discerned in almost all parts of the New Testament: the Kingdom of God will come; it has come: Christ has come; Christ will come. This tension is something which is inseparable from the thought of early Christianity. But whichever way you look at it, it meant that Christians were living in a unique period of history. There had never been anything like it before, and there would not be anything like it again, because, through what had happened, human life had acquired a fresh dimension, and the powers of a world beyond had made impact upon human life in this world.

This is an essential element in the Gospel as it was contained in the primitive *kerygma*. The keynote is already struck in Mark's brief but pregnant summary, "The time is fulfilled, and the Kingdom of God is upon you."

This belief influenced the ethical ideas of early Christianity in two ways.

First, where the sense of impending catastrophe was strong, everything in this world seemed temporary and provisional; only things which would survive the passing of heaven and earth were worthy of attention.

This point of view is put with almost fanatical logic in one of Paul's early letters. "The time," he writes, "is short; so those who have wives should behave as if they had none." What he means by that he explains later on. "The unmarried man," he says, "is concerned about the Lord; he is anxious to please the Lord. The married man is concerned about worldly things; he is anxious to please his wife; and so he has a divided mind." To resume:

Those who have wives [he writes] should behave as if they had none; those who are in trouble should behave as if they had nothing to trouble them; those who rejoice, as if they had nothing to give them joy. If you buy anything, you should remember you do not have it to keep. If you make use of this world's goods, remember you have no chance to use them up, for the structure of this world is passing away. (I Corinthians 7:29–34)

In such a mood as that, it seemed unlikely that the church should ever produce anything like a code of social ethics; and yet it did produce one, as we have seen. As the over-wrought mood of expectation passed, the real value of this sense of the transience of the world appeared. If you really believe that this whole order of civilization, this whole historical process as we have known it, has no necessary permanence, then what are the things worth caring about?

Take this answer to the question from the First Epistle of Peter: "The end of all things is at hand; *therefore,* be sane and sober and say your prayers; above all, have intense love for one another; be hospitable; and use your gifts in the service of God, that He may be glorified in everything." (I Peter 4:7–11. abridged) Such are the things that are worth caring about, if heaven and earth are about to pass away.

Similarly, when Paul moved away from the impatience of early days, he wrote to the Romans the most considered account of Christian ethics that he had as yet produced. It includes a careful and discriminating discussion of the attitude of Christians to the civil authority, without the least suggestion that the civil authority, with all other worldly things, would shortly disappear. Then he adds,

In all this, you must recognize how critical the time is. It is time to wake from sleep. Your deliverance is nearer now than it was when you first became Christians. The night is far advanced; dawn is near. Let us cast away the deeds of darkness and put on the armor of light." (Romans 13:11-12)

In the Epistle to the Ephesians, the same theme is developed further. The author [1] quotes three lines of a hymn:

> Sleeper, awake;
> Rise from the dead;
> And Christ will dawn upon you.

Then he adds, *"Therefore,* be scrupulously careful about your conduct, like wise men, not fools. Take every advantage of the critical moment; for these are bad times. Do not be foolish, but understand what the Lord's will is." (Ephesians 5:14-17)

The sense of transience, the sense of living at a critical moment, when nothing can be guaranteed permanent, has here come to provide a motive for moral earnestness and a sober sense of responsibility. To face the truth that this world, however long or however short may be its course, is essentially transient enables us to contemplate the ultimate ethical demand as absolute claim upon us, whatever temporary and provisional forms it may take. The acknowledgment of that truth is a permanent feature of all sound Christian thinking.

---

[1] It is not agreed whether the Epistle to the Ephesians was actually written by Paul or by a disciple of his. For our present purpose the question is not important.

Perhaps in the present age we are more conscious than our immediate predecessors were that there is no inherent permanence in our existing civilization or in the historical order as a whole. It is well to remind ourselves that it is not in the last resort for the sake of "democracy," or social security, or civilization, that the Christian virtues are important and obligatory upon us, however useful they may be for these ends. Christian virtues were not created, and they are not defined, by the needs of anything so essentially transient. Even if it should turn out (which God in His mercy forbid) that we fail to save our civilization from catastrophe, the fundamental obligations stand fast. "To do justly, to love mercy, and to walk humbly with God," —these are things whose value does not depend upon any transient system. "The world," writes John, "is passing away, and the world's desire, but he who does God's will abides for ever." (I John 2:17)

Secondly, as the expectation of an immediate end of the world faded under the impact of facts, the church came to appreciate more fully the crucial significance of what had already happened. Whatever else might be about to happen, "the age to come," that altogether new period in man's history which had been the goal of so much expectation, really had come. The author of the Fourth Gospel found a formula which by way of paradox, does justice to the situation. He repeats it again and again: "The hour is coming, and *is now*." What was essential in the great expectation was already realized. God was confronting men in a new way. His justice and mercy were realities in human experience, as never before, in view of what Christ had done, and what He had suffered, and what the outcome was of it all. The consequence was that the heights and depths of the moral possibilities of human nature were laid bare. Within the workaday precepts which the church put forth, there lay the potentiality of immensely more exigent moral demands and more efficacious moral resources than men had thought of before.

This opening up of new moral possibilities is not simply an enhanced moral idealism, still less an impracticable perfectionism. It is the recognition that an unattainable ideal lays infinite obligations upon us; that the best we can do lies under the judgment of God; but that the judgment of God carries forgiveness within it. Such forgiveness is not just comfort for the uneasy conscience, but new, originating power. It is in this sense, among others, that Paul describes the Christian life as a "new creation"; that Peter and John speak of "rebirth"; and that the Epistle to the Hebrews declares that through what Christ has done we have entered into "the very heavens," where eternal sacrifice for sin secures eternal pardon.

This conviction of a new order of relations between God and man, involving new heights and depths of moral experience, is a postulate of Christian ethics. In the light of it the whole ethical process receives a new character, since at every point in it we are thrown back upon repentance and faith in God. There will be more to say about this theme when we come to consider the teaching of Jesus in the Gospels.

2. *The Body of Christ.*—A second outstanding feature of the ethical teaching of the early church, as we gather it from the epistles, is the pervasive sense of the organic nature of the community. The church is a body; those who

belong to it are "members" of the body. The term "member" has become watered down in meaning in our common usage. We talk about "members" of a society or club, meaning no more than that the person's name is on the books; but as Paul used the term he was thinking of a living body, with its limbs and organs. These are the "members" of the body. He meant the term in that realistic sense. As such, it provides a powerful ethical motive. In the epistles those who belong to the church are enjoined to practice the social virtues "because we are members one of another." In a classical passage of one of his letters (I Corinthians 12:12–27) Paul expounds in detail and with new force the idea of the body and its members; in other words, the idea of a social organism.

This idea of the community as an organism in which the individuals are members (limbs and organs) of the body, is not peculiar to Christianity. Contemporary Stoics made much of the idea of the social organism, and they freely used the figure of the body and the members. There is a familiar story in the Roman historian Livy about a general strike at Rome in the early days of the republic. The whole of the working class threw down their tools and retired from the city. A member of the government, Menenius Agrippa, went out to negotiate with the strikers. Once upon a time, he told them, the hands and feet rebelled against the stomach. They would no longer spend their time fetching and carrying for such an idle member. So they stopped work; whereupon the whole body fell ill. On hearing this fable, so the story goes, the strikers went back to work. (The world was very young then). Livy has made Menenius Agrippa talk good Stoicism.

So far, then, Paul is following a well-established convention in talking about the community under the figure of the body and its members. But it is a different matter when he insists that this body is "the body of Christ." That actual expression was apparently coined by Paul, but the idea is in no way peculiar to him. Thus, John speaks, not, indeed, of the body and its members, but of a vine and its branches. In the First Epistle of Peter, again, the metaphor is that of a building. The members of the church are "living stones" (as the writer somewhat oddly puts it), built into a structure in which Christ is the "head-stone of the corner," and which thus becomes a temple for the worship of God (I Peter 2. 4–5).

For all these writers, the whole ethical life of Christians takes place within a social organism which is not self-contained or self-complete; a community which is a body only because it is Christ's body, depends upon Him, and serves His ends.

It is obvious that this means a shift in the idea of social obligation. It is a shift which has real importance for some of our present-day problems. Now, as always, there is tension in our thinking between the idea of the individual as an end in himself, self-determining and free, and the idea of the community with its communal ends overriding those of any individual. In some quarters the stress laid upon the community is so strong that the significance of the individual as a moral unit is virtually denied. He lives only for the ends of the state. In reaction to this, we have a violent reassertion of the rights of the individual over against the state, which must end in anarchy as the other ends in tyranny.

The New Testament gives no encouragement to the idea that the individual is self-determining, or is an end in himself. He does not exist for himself. He is a "member" of the body, like a hand or a foot; and, as Paul pertinently points out, if one member suffers, the whole body suffers. You do not say, "My foot has a pain"; you say, *"I* have a pain in my foot." In the same way, if one member of the community suffers, it is the body that suffers. Thus no single one of us, says Paul, can live to himself. He cannot even die to himself. It might seem that if there is any point at which we might reasonably claim some privacy, it is when we die. But according to Paul we belong so completely to the community that even our dying is a public act.

And yet it is not for the community as such that we live or die. It is not for the body, but for Him whose body it is. At this point, I believe, some contemporary statements of Christian ethics fall into error. The individual certainly is not an end in himself, since he exists for God; that is sound Christian doctrine; but there is no Christian warrant for saying that the community as such, any community to which he may happen to belong, has an absolute claim upon the individual. Only the community which is the body of Christ has such a claim, just because it is *Christ's* body. Paul says Christ died "in order that those who live should no longer live to themselves." He does not go on, "but for the church"; he says, "but for Him who died and rose again for them."

Rightly understood, therefore, the church is the one society which can make total demands upon its members without being totalitarian, because it is not, and never claims to be, a self-determining sovereign power. It is entirely subordinate to ends beyond itself, the ends of Christ. Those ends transcend the interest of the church, for Christ is the Savior not of the church alone, but of the world. The church which is His body is interested in the salvation of the world and in no lesser end. Its ultimate reason for existing is the glory of God Himself.

We have now to observe that this conception of the Christian community as the framework for ethical action arises directly out of the Gospel as it was proclaimed from the first. In dying and rising again, it was held, Christ had acted vicariously, or, more properly, had acted as representative of the whole people of God, that is to say, of humanity itself, made anew as God intends it to be. Consequently the community of His followers which emerged out of the crisis was, in however humble a guise, the nucleus of a new humanity, because it had been "crucified with Christ" and had risen with Him. The form of expression is Paul's, but the belief that underlies it was the belief of the whole church from the beginning. In that profoundly religious conviction the Christian doctrine of community, with the social ethic arising out of it, is grounded.

To express what is most characteristic of the Christian life as thus lived within the body of Christ, Paul invented a new phrase. He speaks of men being "in Christ." That phrase is often said to connote "Christ-mysticism," as if it implied a kind of absorption or identification with Christ, like the absorption or identification with the Divine of which the mystics speak. Paul's meaning, however, was much simpler. If a man is a member of Christ's body, then he is "in Christ," whose body it is. To be "in Christ" is to be a member of the church; not, of course, to have your name on the books, but to be in a real sense a limb or organ of Christ's body, dependent upon Him, subject to His will, dedicated to His ends. This fact of being "in Christ," that is to say, being effectively members of His body, which is the church, transforms social relations and the duties they involve.

In the rather academic phraseology which Paul sometimes uses, he describes social relationships on their natural, ordinary level (when they are not "in Christ") as being "in the flesh" (an expression which does not necessarily carry any moral condemnation with it). But after being newly created in Christ, he says, "I henceforth know no one after the flesh." In other words, social relationships are not what they were before; they are transformed by being placed in the context of the Christian society. They are not "in the flesh"; they are "in Christ"; that is to say, they exist within His body. What this may mean, some examples will show.

In the Epistle to Philemon, Paul writes asking his friend to take back a slave who had robbed him and run away. "Receive him," he writes, "no longer as a slave, but as a beloved brother, both in the flesh and in the Lord." The relation of master and servant (a relation belonging to the natural order of society, and therefore "in the flesh") is transformed by being placed in the context of the peculiar kind of community which is the body of Christ.

Again, children are to obey their parents "in the Lord" (Ephesians 6:1). The phrase is far from being conventional. Paul means that within the Christian society, so far as it is truly Christian, the whole relation between parents and

children transcends the natural or instinctive level. Parent
and child are alike "members of Christ." The character
of the child's obedience will be determined by that fact.
It is a different *kind* of obedience. But obedience it is:
there is no New Testament sanction for the view that
children should be brought up to do as they please.

Similarly he writes, "Wives, accept subordination [2] to
your husbands as is fitting in the Lord" (Colossians 3:18).
Many moderns violently repudiate any suggestion of the
subordination of the wife in marriage. Before, however,
dismissing the whole idea, it is worth while to reflect that
Paul is speaking of a peculiar *kind* of subordination,
namely, that which is "in Christ"; that kind of subordination which is in place (or "fitting") where both husband
and wife are "members of Christ."

It is true that Paul has not here worked out in detail
what that kind of subordination is. But in a very remarkable passage of the Epistle to the Ephesians he [3] has worked
out fairly clearly what he conceives to be the proper relation of a husband to his wife, "in Christ."

Husbands [he writes] love your wives as Christ loved the
church and gave Himself for it. . . . Husbands should love
their wives as their own bodies. He who loves his wife loves
himself. No one ever hated his own flesh; he always fosters
and cherishes it—just as Christ loves and cherishes the church
because we are members of His body. . . . That is how each

[2] "Sub-ordination," rather than "subjection," is the word, the
idea being that within the Body there is an "order" befitting its
nature.

[3] Or, it may be, a pupil of his expressing the apostle's thought.
See p. 30.

of you should love his own wife as himself. (Ephesians 5:25–33, abridged)

We observe that an entirely new conception of the marriage relation is emerging, dependent directly upon the central convictions of the Gospel.

3. *The Imitation of Christ.*—Since the church is thus one with Christ as the body with its head, it follows that its members are to find in Him an objective standard of ethical conduct. Says Peter,[4] "He left us an example, that we should follow His steps." Says Paul, "Be imitators of me as I am of Christ (I Corinthians 11:1; similarly, I Thessalonians 1:6, "imitators of us and of the Lord"). In the Fourth Gospel Christ says, "I have set you an example, that you should do as I have done to you" (John 13:15).

The meaning of this is, in the first place, quite simple: if you observe the way in which Jesus behaved in certain situations, into which His followers might also be brought, then you have before you a model of the right way to behave in such situations. Thus, in the passage of the First Epistle of Peter (2:21), to which I have referred, the author is encouraging slaves who are ill treated by their masters by the example of Christ who bore ill treatment without resentment or retaliation. Again, Paul refers to "the gentleness and forbearance of Christ" as an example of the way in which disputes between Christians should be conducted, in particular the sharp dispute in which he was at that moment involved at Corinth (II Corinthians 10:1).

[4] I use the name for the author of the work known as the First Epistle of Peter, without intending to decide whether or not it is actually from the apostle's pen, a question which is not important for our immediate purpose.

On that level, we have a perfectly simple reference to a human example which can be more or less directly copied. In a somewhat similar way, Stoic preachers of the period would appeal to the example of Socrates.

But there is more in the principle of the imitation of Christ than this simple reference to a human example. For instance, in one of his letters to Corinth, Paul appeals to his readers to subscribe generously to the famine-relief fund he was promoting, and he adds, "You know how graciously the Lord Jesus, though He was rich, became poor for our sake, in order that we might grow rich through His poverty" (II Corinthians 8:9). Clearly he does not mean that Jesus was a rich man who gave up his wealth and adopted a life of poverty, like (let us say) Francis of Assisi. No doubt He had a moderately prosperous carpenter's business at Nazareth and sacrificed it for a career which sometimes left Him with nowhere to lay His head; but that could not fittingly be described as being rich and then becoming poor. No, Paul is alluding to the belief of the church that Christ had at His disposal the power and riches of another world, and that He chose the lot of a man, and a poor man at that, in order that He might share those riches of another world with His fellowmen.

This comes out still more clearly in a passage in which Paul writes to persuade the Christians of Philippi to abandon the party spirit and petty ambitions which are threatening to disrupt the church. Once again, he refers them to the example of Christ, "who, though He had the form of God, did not strive for equality with God, but emptied Himself, and, in assuming a human likeness, took the form of a slave; in human shape, He made Himself low and was obedient even unto death, the death of crucifixion" (Philippians 2:5–8).

There is a hard core of historical fact here; Jesus was crucified, and He went to His death in complete obedience to the will of God, like a servant whose only thought is to do what his master wants done. (He had said as much Himself: "The Son of Man came not to be served but to serve, and to give His life.") That stands as a human example. But the apostle sees this act of Jesus as the concrete expression in history of a divine act of self-giving beyond space and time, eternal in its significance, revealing the character of God Himself.

There is here a principle of great importance for Christian ethics. The idea that man should imitate God, or should become as like God as possible, is a very widespread ethical conception. It was part of the preaching both of Greek moralists and of the teachers of Judaism. But it can be a very dangerous maxim. If you heard it said of someone that 'he behaves like a little god,' you would not take it for praise. Self-deification is a temptation that lies in wait for all those who seek to exert great influence over their fellows, even for the best ends. The counsel to imitate God, therefore, or to become like God, is one that we have to use with very great caution, because we really do not know how to translate our conceptions of divine perfection into canons of human behavior.

The New Testament idea of the imitation of Christ is a way of making explicit what *kinds* of divine activity should be imitated by men, and how, and why, and in what circumstances. Thus, Paul is able to say, "Be imitators of God like dear children," adding, "and walk in love

as Christ loved you" (Ephesians 5:2). It is in respect of
the love which Christ showed to man that the character
and action of God are to be copied. To follow His steps
is to have before us a truly human example, but it is also
to have the divine pattern made comprehensible and
imitable. Hence, the imitation of Christ, being the imitation of God Himself so far as God can be a model to His
creatures, becomes a mode of absolute ethics.

4. *The Primacy of Love, or Charity.*—This leads to the
fourth principal motive of Christian ethics, according to
the New Testament; namely, the idea of love, or charity,
as the foundation of all ethical conduct. Here we are in
difficulty about the use of words, because the Greek word
agapé, which is employed in the New Testament, is strictly
untranslatable. Our translations vary between "love" and
"charity." Both are liable to misunderstanding; the term
"love" because it has gathered about itself a mass of senti-
mentalism which is entirely alien to the Greek word, and
to New Testament thought, and the term "charity" because it has become far too narrow and restricted in common use. Provisionally, we might say that *agapé* (love, or
charity) is energetic and beneficent good will which stops
at nothing to secure the good of the beloved object. It is
not primarily an emotion or an affection; it is primarily
an active determination of the will. That is why it can be
commanded, as feelings cannot.

John, for example, makes the point that *agapé* means
nothing unless it carries with it the willingness to share
what you have with your brother who has none (I John
3:17). Paul says that *agapé* is "the full content of the moral
law," because anyone who acts under its impulse will not

injure his neighbor by stealing, killing, committing adultery, coveting his goods, or in any other way. Conversely, if a man in the full sense loves his neighbor, then there can be no outstanding debt of obligation unfulfilled (Romans 13:8-10).

In a famous chapter of his first letter to the Corinthians, Paul describes *agapé* in terms of psychological attitudes: considerateness, courtesy, modesty, unselfishness, and the like (I Corinthians 13). Again, he says that *agapé* is the constructive principle in society; "love builds up" (I Corinthians 8:1).[5] Again, he says it is "the bond of perfection" in the community (Colossians 3:14). The context in which the latter expression is used is worth examining. Paul is here emphasizing the inclusiveness of the Christian community. It comprehends in itself Greek and Jew, circumcized and uncircumcized, barbarian and Scythian, slave and free. All are included within the Christian church. Paul is, however, under no illusion about the difficulty of maintaining effective unity in such a motley society. In this letter, as elsewhere, he lays immense stress on the qualities of character necessary for such unity: compassion, kindliness, humility, gentleness, endless patience, tolerance, and a readiness to forgive as Christ forgave. Then he adds, surprisingly enough, "Over and above all these, clothe yourselves with charity, which is the bond of perfection"; as much as to say that community life, for all that compassion, kindliness and tolerance can do, remains imperfect unless there is real *agapé* between its members. Evidently *agapé*

[5] Is it necessary to add a warning against the traditional translation "edifieth"—a word which in its modern usage is thoroughly misleading?

is something which is beyond even these desirable attitudes of mind to which he has referred, something which will give substance, power, and permanence to such qualities, which in most of us, unfortunately, are so evanescent.

In the end, it is not a virtue among other virtues to which men can aspire. It is that total attitude which is brought about by exposure to the love of God as it is expressed in Christ's self-sacrifice. God made known His love to us through Christ: we were sinners, and Christ died for us. To place ourselves under the effect of that divine act is to have "God's *agapé* diffused in our own hearts" (See Romans 5:5–8). It is put more briefly and crisply in the First Epistle of John; "We love because He loved us first" (not, you will observe, "We love *Him* because He loved us first"). We are capable of love, of *agapé,* at all, only because we are first its objects.

It appears, then, that the governing concept of Christian ethics, love or charity, cannot be understood except out of the Gospel. It shows itself in unselfishness, in courtesy, kindness, compassion, and tolerance; it may go to the lengths of self-sacrifice: yet it *is* none of these things, not even the last, since Paul says it is quite possible for a man to give away all his property, and to die at the stake, and yet not to have *agapé* (I Corinthians 13:3). It is to be defined only in terms of what the Gospel shows of the action of divine charity in Christ.

At this point, then, the religious and the ethical moments in Christianity are no longer distinguishable. Ethics reaches out into that which transcends ethics, while at the same time the religious principle which is the foundation of all Christian theology, the definition of the nature of God himself, cannot be stated except in ethical terms: "God is love." The thing we have to guard against is the danger of converting that proposition simply and saying, "Love is God," making the ethical primary and subordinating the religious to it. If we do that, we are making it impossible ever to understand the thought of the New Testament either on its religious or on its ethical side. For the writer whom I have just quoted there is no possible separation of Gospel and commandment. The theme of both is *agapé,* love, charity, and both together constitute "the word of life" (see I John 1:1; 2:7–10; 4:7–16).

3 · The Ethical Teaching
of the Gospels

WE HAVE REVIEWED four principal points in the ethical teaching of the early church at which the conventional pattern of workaday ethics is given new content and significance by the introduction of distinctive motives. A study of these motives showed that the Christian ethic has its distinctive character from the fact that at the crucial points it is directly related to Christ, and in particular to the work which He accomplished through His death and resurrection; that is to say, it is related to the facts of the Gospel as proclaimed in the *kerygma*.

We have now to notice a further way in which the ethical teaching of the church receives a distinctive stamp from a reference to Christ. I mean the way in which it is directly related to the teaching of Jesus Himself as it was handed down.

Two examples will serve to illustrate the importance which was attached to the tradition of the sayings of the Lord by early Christian teachers. Both of them come from the letters of Paul, who was, we may recall, a highly original and independent thinker, and claimed and exercised substantial authority over the churches he had founded.

In writing to the Corinthians, Paul discusses various questions bearing upon marriage and the relations of the sexes. In the course of the discussion he draws a clear distinction between his own opinion on such questions (which, as we have seen, was sometimes based on rather questionable assumptions [1] though it is never negligible), and the "commandment of the Lord," which is absolutely authoritative (I Corinthians 7:8–12, 25, 40). The particular "commandment" which he cites, forbidding divorce, is contained, in somewhat different verbal forms, in each of the first three Gospels.

In another passage of the same letter he discusses the question of Christian preachers taking pay for their services. After offering certain arguments in favor (which may have sounded more convincing to the first readers than they do to us), he clinches the matter by recalling that "the Lord gave instructions that those who preach the Gospel should make a living out of the Gospel" (I Corinthians 9:14). The saying to which he refers appears in the Gospels in two slightly different verbal forms: in Luke, "The worker deserves his pay"; in Matthew, "The worker deserves his keep."

From these two passages, apart from other less direct but quite cogent evidence, we conclude, first, that the early church possessed a tradition of the sayings of Jesus at a date earlier than the composition of the Gospels; secondly, that this tradition was so firmly established and so universally accepted that appeal to it was final; thirdly, that while the sayings were acknowledged as authoritative in substance, the precise wording was not necessarily fixed, since in each of these cases we have at least three different verbal forms of the same saying; and, fourthly, that some at least of these traditional sayings were later embodied in our Gospels.

[1] See pp. 28–29.

The existence of this preliterary tradition of the teaching of Jesus being established, we can trace its influence in numerous passages of the catechetical teaching of the church where there is no such express reference to it as there is in the passages to which I have just referred, but where nevertheless there is a perfectly distinct echo of the teaching as we know it from the Gospels.

For example, in the Epistle to the Romans we have the maxim "Bless those who persecute you; bless and curse not" (12:14), which clearly echoes a familiar saying in the Sermon on the Mount. We may observe in passing that this saying was current in tradition in several different verbal forms, as we know both from the New Testament and from sources outside the New Testament where it is quoted.

Again, in the same letter Paul is discussing the question of the attitude which the Christian should take towards the pagan government of the Empire, a question which might very well be a matter of life and death for any individual Christian in Rome. Paul says, "Pay all their due; tribute to whom tribute is due, tax to whom tax is due" (Romans 13:7). He does not expressly cite the authority of Jesus for that, but it is hard not to believe that he had in mind the saying in the Gospels, "Pay Caesar what is Caesar's."

To take another example, in writing to the Colossians he says, "Forgive one another, if anyone has a complaint against anyone else; as the Lord forgave you, do likewise." (3:13) That maxim clearly recalls several sayings of Jesus, one of His parables (Matthew 18:21–35), and a clause in the Lord's Prayer.[2]

[2] Observe how in this case a Christian ethical precept has a two-

But perhaps the most interesting and illuminating passage of this kind is the long discussion upon the question of food taboos, or the distinction between "clean" and "unclean" foods, which we have in the fourteenth chapter of the Epistle to the Romans. In a church which included a considerable number of Jews in its membership, it was natural that this question of the continued validity of the Jewish food laws should arise, and should be vigorously disputed. Paul lays down the principle that there is no inherent "uncleanness" in any food at all. "I am convinced," he says, "in the Lord Jesus, that nothing is unclean in itself." We recall that a statement to that effect is reported as a saying of Jesus in the Gospels: "Nothing that enters into a man from outside can make him unclean; it is what comes out of him that makes him unclean"; to which Mark adds, "Thus He made all foods clean" (Mark 7:14-19). It is incredible that Paul was not aware of this saying. As a piece of corroborative evidence, I would remark that the Greek term which is used for "unclean" (*koinos*) is an unusual and peculiar word to use in that sense, and Paul and Mark agree in using it. We may, I think, take it that Paul was acquainted with this saying of the Lord, and that is why he knows he is on firm ground in laying down the general principle (which some of his readers would certainly be reluctant to accept), that no food is inherently unclean.

In the situation which he has in mind, however, that is

---

fold basis: it rests upon the Gospel as an affirmation of what God has done in Christ (see pp. 41–42), and upon express sayings of Jesus incorporated in the tradition of His teaching. This is characteristic of the genius of Christian ethics.

not all that needs to be said. The church is being disturbed by differences in conscientious convictions among its members. We know well what acute dissensions strongly held conscientious convictions can bring about. To ride roughshod over any man's conscientious convictions is morally dangerous, however wrong those convictions may be, and the censoriousness that such disputes bring forth is disastrous to Christian unity. So it was in Rome. "Why do you judge your brother?" asks Paul; "We must all stand before the judgment seat of God"; and again, "Make up your mind never to put an obstacle or a 'scandal' in your brother's way." Surely he was thinking of two sayings of the Lord: the first, "Judge not that you may not be judged, for with what judgment you judge you shall be judged" and the other, that very severe saying of His about "scandalizing" the weaker brother (Matthew 18:6–7; Mark 9:42; Luke 17:1–2). Once again we observe that an unusual Greek word, *skandalon,* is used in both cases. It is "translation Greek"; in fact it is thoroughly bad Greek, which Paul would not naturally have used. He feels it necessary to provide a good Greek word (*proskomma,* "obstacle") to explain it. That, I think, corroborates the view that he is here echoing a traditional saying of Jesus which had been handed down with that peculiar word in it, as we have it in Matthew.

It appears, then, that the whole discussion in the fourteenth chapter of Romans turns upon the exegesis and application of three traditional sayings of Jesus, which were later embodied in our Gospels. But that is not all. In the same passage Paul appeals to the most fundamental convictions of the Gospel, those which have regard to the meaning of the death and resurrection of Christ. "Do not ruin with your food the brother for whom Christ died." "None of us lives to himself and none of us dies to himself. If we live, we live to the Lord, and if we die, we die to the Lord; for this is why Christ died and rose again, to become Lord of living and dead."

The entire passage, then, is a most instructive, and a most impressive, illustration of the way in which the Gospel of Christ and the tradition of the teaching of Jesus are combined in the working out of a Christian ethic for daily life.

We now turn to the sayings of Jesus themselves as they are recorded in the Gospels, and as in substance they lay before the teachers of the early church, to provide both inspiration and a standard of reference. What, we ask, is the character, and what is the intention, of the ethical teaching of Jesus as we have it in the Gospels?

To begin with, if we compare the teaching given in the Gospels with the ethical parts of the Epistles that we have had before us, it seems clear that they are not upon the same level. The Gospels do not give directions for conduct *in the same sense* as do the ethical precepts of the Epistles.

This may, perhaps, best be illustrated by recalling some typical passages. Take such a thoroughly typical piece of early Christian catechetical teaching as the twelfth chapter of Romans:

Be affectionate to one another as members of a family, vying with one another in mutual respect. Be diligent. Be fervent in spirit. Do service to the Lord. Be hopeful and joyous. Be steadfast in time of trouble. Contribute to the needs of Christian people and practice hospitality. Bless those who persecute you; bless instead of cursing. Share your joys and sorrows, and have a common mind.[3]

Now take some of the familiar sayings of Jesus in the Gospels which *prima facie* deal with similar topics.

When you give a luncheon or dinner party, do not invite your friends and relations or your rich neighbors, in case they should invite you in return and you get paid back; but invite beggars, cripples, lame, and blind. That will bring you real happiness, because they can give you nothing in return. (Luke 14:12–13)
If anyone strikes you on the right cheek, turn the other one. If anyone chooses to go to law to get your shirt, let him have your coat as well. If an official puts you to a mile of forced labor, go with him two miles. Give to anyone who asks, and never refuse a request for a loan. (Matthew 5:39–42)

The style, to begin with, is different. The sayings in the Gospels have an incomparably greater liveliness and pungency than the maxims in the *catechesis*. Apart from that, however, it is surely clear that these two sets of precepts are not conceived on the same level. The precepts in Romans are perfectly straightforward general maxims which you could transfer directly to the field of conduct. You could take them quite literally as they stand and try to put them into practice, and the attempt would be worth making. That could hardly be said of the Gospel precepts. Whatever you make of them, you could not profitably go about applying these precepts directly and literally as they stand. It is not that they are necessarily so very difficult—I

[3] For form and style, compare this passage with the extracts given on p. 18.

mean taken literally. In fact, it might be easier to give to every beggar you meet than to exercise discrimination. They are not in that sense difficult. It is that these precepts are simply not suitable, as the precepts in Romans are, for use as a plain guide to conduct, if you take them literally as they stand. Evidently they were not intended for such use.

To get them in their right setting, we must try to envisage the teaching of Jesus as a whole. To do that, it is a good plan to start with the parables. Practically everybody is agreed that the parables taken as a whole bear an unmistakable individual stamp. It is possible that one or two of them may be what is called in art criticism "studio pieces," where pupils have worked on the master's design; but, just as the possibility that a few pictures ascribed to Rubens (let us say), are really studio pieces does not in the least shake our confidence that in general we know a Rubens when we see it, so we may say with confidence that a parable in the gospels is a work of art whose author can rarely be in doubt. They show perfectly definite, recognizable characteristics.

What are these characteristics? First, a poetical and imaginative quality which is quite distinctive. Secondly, the realism and close observation of the pictures which they draw, even in a few strokes. The parables taken together constitute a picture of life in the *petite bourgeoisie* and working classes of a Roman province to which there is scarcely a parallel in the whole literature of the period.[4] Thirdly, there is their dramatic quality, by which I mean

[4] See C. H. Dodd, *The Authority of the Bible,* London, 1938, pp. 147–152.

the way in which the idea, whatever it may be, is expressed in action, concretely; recognizable human action, in a realistic setting.[5]

As regards the parables, I believe everyone will agree that this is so. What is not always sufficiently recognized is that these same qualities, this same poetical, imaginative quality, this same realism, and this same dramatic power pervade virtually the whole of the teaching of Jesus as we have it in the Gospels. It is to be found not only in the parables properly so-called, but also in maxims which *prima facie* are straightforward precepts for action.

No one, for example, supposes that when Jesus says, "When you give alms, do not blow your own trumpet," He is giving instructions about the use of musical instruments. It is a picturesque and dramatic way of saying that alms-giving should not be ostentatious. It is not that the Author of the saying first thought of the principle of non-ostentation and then devised a picture to illustrate it. It is rather that the poetical and dramatic imagination saw it like that from the beginning.

Again, "If you are in the act of making your offering at the altar and suddenly remember that your brother has something against you, leave your offering where it is in front of the altar and go and get reconciled with your brother; then you can come back and make your offering." The meaning might be put in the words, "personal relations are more important than religious observance"; but the truth is presented as it was seen by the Author in a dramatic picture of action. If anyone were so misguided

[5] See C. H. Dodd, *Parables of the Kingdom,* London, 1935, pp. 18–21 *et passim.*

as to try to transfer this dramatic picture directly and literally as it stands to actual life, what hopeless confusion would result! Nor, indeed, am I at all impressed by those who solemnly argue from this passage that Jesus intended to sanction the continued attendance of His disciples at the services of the temple.

Similarly, "If anyone strikes you on the cheek, turn the other cheek." That saying is at home in the same world of dramatic imagination as those we have been considering and it is to be understood in the same way. So are most of the ethical maxims in the Gospel. They are dramatic illustrations which exhibit and illuminate from various angles a consistent outlook on life, a consistent understanding of God, man and the world, which is the background and presupposition of ethical action. What is the key to this outlook, this understanding?

We may begin once again with the parables. It is remarkable what a large number of parables describe some point in a man's experience at which a long-continued process comes to a head and demands decisive action.

The kingdom of God [so the parable runs] is as if a man should sow seed in the earth, and go to sleep and wake, night and day, while the seed is growing, he knows not how. Spontaneously the earth produces a crop: first blade, then ear, and then full corn in the ear. *But when the crop is ready, he sets the sickle to work, because harvest has come.* (See Mark 4:26–29)

Things have come to a head: the man must act.

Again, here is a vineyard, with men working. Some began at crack of dawn, some at the third hour of the day, some at the sixth or the ninth hour. The day is wearing on: it is the eleventh hour—and now it is the twelfth, and the day is over. The men knock off work; the wages are paid (no chance of overtime!) The account is settled. (see Matthew 20:1–16).

Again, rent day has arrived, and the landlord is collecting his dues. Or the creditor is calling in his debts. The dishonest steward's long career of successful fraud has been detected, and he is under notice of dismissal. The master is coming home; no one knows when. His servants are waiting. It is evening—it is midnight—it is cockcrow—it is dawn. Suddenly he is there! But—were they ready? [6]

Again, the shepherd's weary search is over, and the lost sheep is found. The merchant's travels are ended: he has the pearl of price. The missing son is home at long last from the far country, and the dance begins. The wedding day has come; the feast is spread; the word goes round, "Come, for all is ready!" [7]

Thus, parable after parable depicts in vivid and variable imagery the arrival of a "zero hour" in human experience. What, then, is the real zero hour to which all these parables refer, and which they all illustrate or dramatize? The answer is, "The Kingdom of God is upon you." That is what the world was waiting for, as the farmer waits for the harvest, as the household servants waited for the master's return, partly in hope and partly in trepidation. The people whom Jesus addressed in His teachings (this is what He meant) were in the position of all these various characters in the parables. In His coming, in what He said

[6] See Mark 12:1–9; Matthew 18:23–35; Luke 16:1–8; Mark 13:34–36.

[7] See Luke 15:4–6; Matthew 13:45–46; Luke 15:11–24; Matthew 22:1–10.

and did, in the whole train of events which ended in His death and resurrection, men were confronted with the Kingdom of God; that is to say, confronted with God Himself in His kingdom, power, and glory; no absentee, but a present factor in the situation, of which they must take account.

It is, perhaps, necessary at this point to clear up a possible misconception. At one time it was very generally held that the term "the Kingdom of God" in the Gospels was only a rather old-fashioned biblical way of speaking about utopia or the goal of social progress—or any desirable state of things that might appeal to one. That idea still lingers; but that is not what the Gospels mean by the Kingdom of God.

So far as our information goes, Jesus never undertook to say outright what the Kingdom of God *is*. In fact, He was understood to say it was a secret that very few knew (Mark 4:11). But He could tell them what it is *like*. It is like sowing and harvest; it is like a householder who went on a long journey and came back unexpectedly; it is like hidden treasure found; and so on through the whole gallery of pictures from real life that He has drawn.

Often enough, the event which is *like* the Kingdom of God is an unexpected and disconcerting event. In any case, it always calls for decisive action. The farmer can go to sleep and wait night and day while the seed is growing, but when the harvest has come he must set the sickle to work; else the harvest is wasted. The pearl merchant must be ready, there and then, to sell out everything he has got: else he loses his bargain. The dishonest steward who is under notice of dismissal must there and then bestir

himself to find some means, fair or foul, of making a live-
lihood; else he will starve, since he is incapable of digging
and ashamed to beg.

There are some for whom zero hour brings disaster.
There is the craven and overcautious servant who hid his
talent in a napkin. There is the household steward who
instead of attending to his job spent his time, as the Gospels
pungently say, "feasting and getting drunk and beating
up the boys and girls" (Luke 12:45). But in its main intention, the great event means fullfilment and satisfaction.
It is *good* to have the master home again. It is *good* to
possess the pearl of great price, whatever its cost. There is
the wedding feast, music and dancing, harvest-home.
There is the greeting to the faithful servant, "Enter into
the joy of your lord."

All these parables in fact depict the ministry of Jesus
Christ as the great moment when the relations between
God and man were put on a new footing, when the great
moral issues could no longer be shirked, and when the
possibilities of human life were indefinitely enlarged.

Such, then, is the presupposition of the whole of the
teaching of Jesus. It is the presupposition not only of His
moral precepts but of everything that He had to say: what
He had to say, for example, about God's care for His
children ("The very hairs of your head are numbered");
what He had to say about the certainty of God's response
to our need ("Your Father knows that you have need of
all these things. Ask and you will receive; seek and you
will find; knock and the door will be opened"); or again,
what He said about the power of faith in God to "move
mountains," about the certainty of God's victory over all

the powers of evil ("I saw Satan fallen like lightning from heaven"); or again, about the blessedness of the poor, the hungry, the sorrowful, and the persecuted, since "theirs is the Kingdom of God."

In all these sayings there is the vivid, picturesque, dramatic quality that we have already noted. Such sayings as these, along with the parables, go to build up a consistent picture which conveys to the imagination a vivid sense that God is here, no longer a remote Providence, but directly active in the human scene, and that it is impossible to put any limits to His good will towards His creatures, since he is "kind to the unthankful and the evil." Nor is it possible to put any limits to His power to carry this good will into effect since "all things are possible with God." Such are the general outlines of the picture that is set before us, and the ethical precepts may best be understood, in the first instance and in their first intention, as helping to fill out this same picture. For if God is One who numbers our hairs and knows all our needs, He is also One whose moral judgments are inexorable. The immediacy of His care is balanced by the immediacy of His demands upon us.

Such is the setting of the ethical teaching of Jesus. It contemplates human conduct in the most concrete way possible, as related to a real situation in which the one inescapable and overriding fact is the fact of God Himself; a situation, therefore, in which the whole seriousness of the moral predicament of man is laid bare and in which endless possibilities of fullfilment and satisfaction are opened. Consequently it challenges men to decision.

The proclamation with which, we are told, Jesus began

His ministry in Galilee is summarized in the words, "The time is fulfilled; the Kingdom of God is upon you; repent and believe the Gospel." First, there is a declaration of the situation which has come about, without any design or planning on the part of men, simply by act of God. History has reached its climax, and whether they will or no, they must face this situation. It is the zero hour, in which decisive action is called for. The proclamation, therefore, demands a response on the part of men. The desired response is summed up in the words, "Repent and believe the Gospel."

What is here called "believing the Gospel" is not very different from what is elsewhere described as "receiving the Kingdom of God like a child." It means accepting the truth of the situation, simply and frankly, yielding one's self to it, and doing what has to be done about it.

The word "repent" needs a little more consideration. It implies that those to whom it is addressed have been in the wrong. It also implies that they are to be willing to be radically readjusted—not only to behave differently in this or that particular, but to redirect the affections and the will, where the springs of action lie. If such a readjustment is to be made, and made intelligently and therefore with effect, we must appreciate clearly just where things went wrong and what are the true values to which we have to reorientate ourselves. I believe we shall get the ethical teaching of the Gospels into the right perspective if we think of it as providing the material for an intelligent act of "repentance" in this sense. It is not so much detailed guidance for conduct in this or that situation, as a disclosure of the absolute standards which alone are relevant when the Kingdom of God is upon us. These standards, however, are not defined in general and abstract propositions, but in dramatic pictures of action in concrete situations; and they are intended to appeal to the conscience by way of the imagination.

"Give to everyone who asks." "Turn the other cheek." "Leave father and mother, wife and children, and hate your own soul." "If your hand or your eye is leading you astray, cut it off and cast it away." "Never worry about food or drink. The morrow will look after itself." The one thing that all such sayings clearly enforce is the unlimited scope of God's commands. They leave no room for complacency. It is impossible to be satisfied with ourselves, when we try our conduct by these standards; and yet, since God is here in His kingdom, these standards are obligatory. It is put briefly in the maxim; "When you have done every thing say, 'We are unprofitable servants: we have only done our duty'" (Luke 17:10). Such sayings as these invite us to recognize how far away from God's demands our best has been. They provide an objective standard for self-criticism. In other words, they bring home God's judgment upon us. To accept this judgment is the first step in what the New Testament calls "repentance."

These seemingly harsh and uncompromising demands, however, are set within a picture of the Kingdom of God which holds out the prospect of fullfilment and satisfaction beyond all measure, because God is what He is. "Fear not, little flock; it is your Father's good pleasure to give you the Kingdom." Thus, repentance passes from the negative action which is the acceptance of God's judgment upon our evil to the positive realization of new possibilities. The transition from the negative to the positive is what is called in the gospels the forgiveness of sins. I need hardly remind you how large a place forgiveness holds in the gospels, not only in the teaching of Jesus, but even more in the record of His actual dealing with the moral failures of society (the "publicans and sinners" of the gospel narration).

The precepts of Christ, then, in judging us, expose our need for forgiveness and throw us back upon the inexhaustible mercy of God which offers such forgiveness. Forgiveness is clearly not merely a balm to the uneasy conscience; it is the actual creative power of God coming in His kingdom, released for action when men accept His judgment and repent; and it opens up unlimited possibilities to the enterprise of the repentant and forgiven sinner.

At this point the ethical precepts begin to take on a fresh aspect. They become not only the standards by which our conduct is judged, but guideposts on the way we must travel in seeking the true ends of our being under the Kingdom of God.

Although the several precepts cannot, as we have seen, serve as exact rules of behavior in particular situations, yet, taken together, they do set before us an ethical task which is obligatory upon us. In the Gospel according to Matthew the principal body of ethical sayings of Jesus is gathered together in what is called the Sermon on the Mount. It is not without deliberate intention that Matthew has so placed the 'Sermon' as to suggest a parallel with the promulgation of the law of Moses from Mount Sinai, and he has emphasized that parallel by putting together a series of sayings which draw a comparison and contrast between the provisions of the old law and of the new. Jesus, in fact, is here represented as the King who promulgates a new law for His subjects. In some sense, therefore, the ethical precepts of Jesus are intended to constitute a law: in what sense, we shall next consider.

4 · The Law of Christ

WE HAVE SEEN that the ethical precepts of the gospels serve two purposes. On the one hand, they help towards an intelligent and realistic act of "repentance," because they offer an objective standard of judgment upon our conduct, so that we know precisely where we stand in the sight of God, and are in a position to accept His judgment upon us and thereby to partake of His forgiveness. On the other hand, they are intended to offer positive moral guidance for action, to those who have, in the words of the gospels, received the Kingdom of God.

The Sermon on the Mount, which contains so many of these precepts, ends with a parable which leaves no possible doubt that they are intended to be obeyed.

Everyone who hears these sayings of mine and carries them out shall be compared to a prudent man who built his house on the rock. Down came the rain, the floods rose, the winds blew and rushed upon that house, but it did not fall, because it was founded on the rock. And everyone who hears these sayings of mine and does not carry them out shall be compared to a stupid man who built his house on sand. Down came the rain, the floods rose, the winds blew; they struck that house, and it fell; and what a fall it was!

It appears, then, that we shall not be far wrong in taking the Sermon on the Mount as Matthew has represented it —namely, as the new law which supersedes the law of the Old Testament—the law of the Kingdom of God. That, I believe, is the sense in which any reasonable reader would understand the Sermon upon an unprejudiced reading of it. But we have to take account of the fact that in certain quarters of the Church, and I think especially in the churches of the Reformation, there has been a strong bias against any understanding of Christianity as a new law. This bias comes out very strongly in some forms of contemporary neo-Protestantism.

Historically, it is largely based upon certain passages of the Pauline epistles, as they were taken up by the sixteenth-century Reformers. In one place Paul states roundly that "Christ is the end of the law for all who have faith" (Romans 10:4); and in another place, "you are not under law but under grace" (Romans 6:14). He has a great deal to say about "redemption," or, in a less theological rendering of the Greek term (*apolytrosis*), emancipation. If you ask "Emancipation from what?" one answer quite plainly is, "Emancipation from law." He speaks disparagingly of "works of the law" in contrast to faith, through which, alone, he says, we are justified by grace and sanctified by the Spirit.

In apparently logical consistency with such teachings, many Christian theologians, in almost all periods of the Church, and certainly at the present time, have protested against any construction of the Christian religion which, by introducing legal conceptions, seems to blur the splendor of the Gospel as the affirmation of the free and unconditioned grace of God to sinful men or to question the complete adequacy of a life directed inwardly by the Spirit in independence of external authority of any kind. They take the view that in such passages as those that I have quoted Paul is stating the true basis of Christianity, and that other New Testament writers, the evangelist Matthew in particular, represent a descent of the Church into a new legalism.

Since, then, the school to which I have referred appeals to Paul, to Paul let us go. In spite of all his anti-legal sentiments, Paul acknowledged himself to be "within Christ's law" (I Corinthians 9:21), and he called upon his converts to "fullfil the law of Christ" (Galatians 6:2). He settled disputed points of conduct by citing a "commandment of the Lord." Believing himself to have received authority from Christ, he gave "orders" to his converts, and unequivocally demanded obedience. When his orders were questioned by persons claiming to have the Spirit or to be prophets, he turned upon them peremptorily. "If anyone thinks," he writes, "that he is a prophet or an inspired person, he must recognize that what I write is the Lord's command. If he is ignorant of that, he can be ignored" (I Corinthians 14. 37–38).

It is not, then, so clear, after all, that Paul intended to repudiate the understanding of Christianity as a new law. We must look more closely.

We recall that the earliest form in which Christianity was presented to the world, so far as we can discover, was two-fold: it consisted of the proclamation (*kerygma*), which declared what God has done for men, and the teaching (*didaché*), which declared what God expects man to do. I suggested that there was a real analogy here to the basic formula of the religion of the Old Testament. The Decalogue begins with the proclamation, "I am the Lord, thy God, who brought thee out of the land of Egypt," declaring what God had done; and it goes on to lay down the fundamental commands of the moral law—what man is expected to do. The Decalogue, and indeed the whole Torah, or Law of Moses, was regarded as the document of a "covenant" between God and His people. A covenant is what we call a "bilateral agreement." Of course, there can be no question of a negotiated agreement on equal terms between the Creator and His creatures. The initiative lies with God alone, and He alone defines the terms of agreement, which, indeed, proceed directly from His own character, His purpose for mankind, and the historical action in which that purpose is expressed and fullfilled. And yet, it is of the essence of the contract that man should accept these terms. Man, therefore, is not a passive recipient, but an active party to the covenant, who undertakes the obligations which it lays upon him. So much we may learn from the Old Testament.

In the New Testament, the Christian religion is represented as a "new covenant." Like the old covenant, it rests upon a divine initiative. As the old covenant rested upon the act of God in delivering Israel from Egypt, so the new covenant rests upon the act of God in redeeming mankind through the death and resurrection of Christ. As the old covenant laid upon Israel consequential obligations which were defined in the Decalogue, and more explicitly in the whole law of Moses, so the new covenant lays consequential obligations upon the Church. The nature of these obligations corresponds to the nature of the act of God by which the new covenant was instituted. Ultimately, therefore, it corresponds to the character and purpose of God Himself.

It is clear that for early Christians this parallel with the covenant of Sinai threw real light upon the situation in which they found themselves in the Church, as a result of God's redemptive act in Christ. But they were aware that the parallel was only partial, because this was a *new* covenant. The Old Testament itself pointed to certain features in which a new covenant must be in contrast with the old.

In the sixth century B.C., when the earlier system of Judaism collapsed at the Babylonian conquest, the prophet Jeremiah had declared that, the old covenant having now become void through the breach of its terms by the Jewish people, God would institute a new covenant. Under the terms of this new covenant, the sins of the past would be forgiven, and they would "know God" in quite a new way, because His law would be "written on their hearts" instead of upon tables of stone (Jeremiah 31:31–34).

This feature of the new covenant, the law written on the heart, is what struck the imagination of Paul. In the third chapter of his second letter to the Corinthians he draws the contrast of the two covenants in detail. He speaks here of an "epistle of Christ, inscribed not with ink but with the spirit of the living God, not upon tablets of stone, but upon hearts of flesh for tablets." [1] While the old covenant, he says, was an "administration of the written word," the new covenant is an "administration of the spirit." The contrast of the "written word" and the "spirit" is central and crucial to the conception of the Christian

---

[1] Paul's use of the metaphor is slightly confused, if one attempts to work it out in detail, but his general meaning is sufficiently clear.

law, and it is important to enquire what is the precise contrast intended.

The expression which I have rendered "written word," in Greek *gramma,* is translated in our current versions "letter." The translation comes through the Latin, but it is not an accurate rendering of the meaning of the Greek: *gramma* means a written document. There is a certain misconception which has sometimes seriously confused the issue in this passage. It was supposed that the "letter" stood for the literal meaning of the Old Testament, and the "spirit" for an allegorical interpretation by which obsolete provisions of the Law of Moses (for example) might be given artificial meanings edifying to Christians. It was probably an unlucky day for Christian theology when Bishop Ambrose of Milan persuaded the young Augustine, later to become the great teacher of western Christendom, that the maxim, "The letter killeth but the spirit maketh alive" (in II Corinthians 3:6) meant that the literal sense of the Old Testament is dangerous, but that an allegorical interpretation makes it safe and profitable for Christians. In any case, that is not Paul's intention.

His description of the Law of Moses as *gramma,* a written document, is tolerably clear (though he has pardonably confused an inscription on stone with a document written in ink). Each commandment, he means, in the law of Moses is set down (as we say) in black and white, with all necessary precision, ready to be transferred directly to the field of daily conduct. In this it is typical of all systems of ethics which present a code of rules and regulations to be carried out "to the letter." It is, as he carefully defines it elsewhere, a "law of commandments contained in ordinances" (Ephesians 2:15). As such, he holds, it is abolished in Christ. In its place is a law "written on the heart."

What that means, is not so immediately clear. In some sense, no doubt, it is inward, while the "law of commandments contained in ordinances" is external. But that is an ambiguous way of speaking, and I suspect it has led to a good deal of misunderstanding. Paul certainly did not mean to say that there is no law for the Christian except his own "inner light." "To every man his own conscience is God": that sentiment, I believe, would be widely applauded as a fine statement of the Christian doctrine of the freedom, or autonomy, of the individual. Actually, it is a sentiment of the pagan poet Menander, and it is at variance with the fundamental Christian position that the Lord is King and the conscience of man His subject.

It is, indeed, difficult to maintain, in face of the New Testament, the once-popular view that Christianity is a "religion of the spirit" in a sense which contrasts it with "religions of authority." Its basic postulate is the Kingdom of God; and a kingdom implies authority. Such authority was, according to the Gospels, claimed by Jesus Christ in His ministry. It was, in fact, a conflict about authority that led to His death. He taught, we are told, "with authority, and not as the scribes"; and certainly the note of authority is everywhere present in His sayings, with their emphatic "I say unto you"—a form of speech which has often been noted as a counterpart to the "Thus saith the Lord" of the Old Testament prophets. Clearly, then, it would be a mistake to think that the difference between the "administration of the written word" and the "administration of the spirit" is precisely that between objective and subjective ethical standards, or between authority and freedom.

Let us make a fresh start from the idea of the "covenant" itself. That idea, we have seen, carries with it the implications, first, that God has done something for men, which initiates the covenant, and, secondly, that it entails consequential obligations. What God has done for men is variously described in the New Testament, but perhaps most succinctly and effectively in the well-known verse of the Fourth Gospel, which says: "God so loved the world that He gave His only Son, in order that whoever has faith in Him should not perish but have eternal life" (John 3:16).

This classical statement acquaints us with three things. It tells us not only what God did (He gave His Son), but also what is the *quality* of His act and what is its *direction* or purpose. Its quality is that of love, or charity—the untranslatable *agapé;* and it was directed towards the perfection of life in God's creation—eternal life. This act of *agapé* is conceived as realized and completed in the self-sacrifice of Christ. In the same gospel, Christ, in the very act of devoting Himself to death for the salvation of man, addresses His followers thus: "I have set you an example, that you should do as I have done to you . . . I give you a new commandment: love one another. As I have loved you, you are to love one another." (John 13:15, 34) Here, then, is the basic statement of the obligation which the new covenant entails, in consequence of the divine action by which it was initiated. It is an obligation to reproduce in human action the *quality* and the *direction* of the act of God by which we are saved.

It might appear that at this point we could go on at once to answer our question about the law "written on the heart," or the "law of the spirit," as distinct from the external "law of commandments contained in ordinances." May we not say that this inward law has one provision, namely, that in everything we do we should act in the spirit of love; or, as Augustine put it, "Love and do as you please"?

Augustine's maxim has the value of a challenging epigram, but it can be seriously misleading. It is too much exposed to the danger of a barren sentimentality, which is far removed from the temper of the New Testament. The teachers of the early church certainly were not content to leave it at that. The First Epistle of John brings it down to earth in this author's crude and pedestrian way. He writes, "If anyone possesses the means of earthly existence and sees his brother in want, and shuts his heart against him, how can the divine charity dwell in him?" (I John 3:17) Accordingly, these early Christian teachers went to the trouble of drawing up a comprehensive and somewhat detailed scheme of ethical teaching carefully related, as we have seen, to the actual structure of contemporary society and its demands, and they gave it force and vitality by referring it, at all the crucial points, to the fundamental quality and direction of the divine act by which we are saved, as it is declared in the Gospel. But that is not all. As we have seen, Jesus Himself set forth a substantial number of ethical precepts, and these precepts are couched in markedly authoritative tone, and are accompanied by solemn warnings that they are intended to be obeyed.

Let us look again at some of the actual precepts of Jesus.

They are not—so much is agreed—a "law of command-ments contained in ordinances," inasmuch as few of them are capable of being made into direct regulations for be-havior, enforceable, if necessary, by judicial or disciplinary measures. In this they differ markedly from much of the contemporary rabbinic teaching, which aimed precisely at producing a foolproof scheme of rules and regulations in obedience to which man might conform to the law of God in all likely contingencies.

Yet the precepts of Jesus are very far from being mere broad generalities. They deal with highly concrete situa-tions: an insolent fellow slaps you in the face; an im-portunate beggar keeps asking for more; you are giving a dinner party and wondering whom to invite. The pre-cepts are far from general; they are even embarrassingly specific in the kind of conduct they enjoin: "turn the other cheek!" "Give to everyone who asks!" "Do not invite your rich acquaintances, but have a party of beggars and crip-ples!" The terms "paradox" and "hyperbole" are often used in speaking of such precepts. If we take those terms to denote nothing more than figures of speech or rhetori-cal devices to give emphasis or stimulate reflection, we are not going deep enough. Jesus certainly intended His pre-cepts to be taken seriously.

I suggest that we may regard each of these precepts as indicating, in a dramatic picture of some actual situation, the *quality* and *direction* of action which shall conform to the standard set by the divine *agapé*. The quality may be present in its degree at a quite lowly level of achieve-ment. The right direction may be clearly discernible in the act, even though the goal may be still far off. But the demand that our action in concrete situations shall have *this* direction and *this* quality is categorical.

Take for example that injunction to turn the other cheek. It is hardly possible to treat it as a ruling to be directly applied in all appropriate circumstances. It is not only that we may not be good enough to put it into practice, but it may not be, in the confused and distorted state of human affairs in which we live, always the best thing to do. On the other hand, it can hardly be regarded as the ideal of conduct in an ideally perfect society. In such a society, I suppose, there would be no people going about slapping other people's faces, and the contingency would not arise. But the picture which Jesus here draws sets before us vividly, in the context of an imperfect society like the one we live in, the patience, the detachment from egoism and pride, and the respect for other people, however objectionable, which we can clearly see to conform to God's action towards us in Christ. We are to imitate, in our measure, His forbearance under affronts, His respect for our freedom which will not allow Him to coerce, and His endless patience. And these qualities must give character to Christian action, even at a lowly level; even if all we can manage is a half-frustrated effort to overcome, or at least to moderate, our natural pride, resentment, and impatience, for Christ's sake. In making that effort, if it is honestly made, we have obeyed the command of Christ, since the very effort has in it the quality and moves in the direction, which He prescribes, while every such effort will help us to realize afresh the immense distance which still separates us from perfect fullfilment of His law.

Let us try to get clear exactly where the difference lies

between such precepts as this and a code of regulations. Take as example one such regulation from the law of Moses, which, as it happens, Jesus Himself selected as a basis for His criticism of the Pharisees: the law of tithe, that is, the rule that a tenth part of all produce of the land should be dedicated to God (In an agricultural society, that meant a tenth part of every man's gross income). The true ethical basis of this law is the very important principle that no one has absolute right of disposal over any commodities—or over money, the equivalent of commodities—which may come into his possession. As a symbolic expression of that principle, the rule was made that everyone should devote a token sum of 10 percent of his gross income to religious or charitable purposes, exactly as the law of the land levies a certain proportion for income tax.

Such a rule as that can be either obeyed or disobeyed, and the line between obedience and disobedience is perfectly sharp and clear. If you assign to these purposes less than 10 percent, you have disobeyed the law. If you assign precisely 10 percent, you have fulfilled the law; there is no more to be said. If you choose to devote 12 percent, that is your own affair. Now, as Jesus pointed out, it is perfectly possible to keep that law with the most scrupulous precision, to such a pitch that you devote to God every tenth sprig of mint in your garden, and yet not to come within hailing distance of "the weightier matters of the law," which He defined as "justice, mercy, and the love of God." [2]

It is important to notice precisely what it is that He

[2] So Luke 11:42; in Matthew 23:23 it is "justice, mercy and faith."

says. "These things" (namely, justice, mercy, and the love of God) "are what you ought to have done, and at the same time you ought not to leave the others undone" (namely, the tithing of your produce). In other words, it is a good thing to have exact rules to follow, and if you have them, it is a good thing to follow them conscientiously, but all this may have little to do with fundamental morals, with justice, mercy, and the love of God.

In contrast to the law of tithe, consider some of the precepts that Jesus laid down about money and its use. "You cannot serve God and property." "Do not accumulate capital on earth." "No one who does not renounce everything he has got can be my disciple." "Sell all you have and give alms, and so provide yourselves with purses that will never wear out." "Give to everyone who asks."

Clearly, it is impossible ever to say, categorically, that you *have kept* such precepts as these in their full scope; and yet, if you take them seriously at all, they will make themselves felt in every single thing you do that is concerned with the disposal of your money. They are not vague or ambiguous. Approaching the conscience through the imagination, they make abundantly clear what must be the quality of every action that has to do with money, and in what direction it must tend, and that quality and that direction may be recognizable in actions that are trivial, or imperfect, or even mistaken. In so far as that is so, Christ's precepts have been obeyed; and yet they are not fulfilled, because they open up vistas towards an unattainable and even inconceivable perfection.

Consequently, you can never say of the precepts of Christ, as a certain rich man said about the Ten Commandments,

"All these I have kept from my youth." We are at least saved from the morally dangerous state of complacency and self-righteousness. "A good conscience," said Albert Schweitzer, "is an invention of the devil." The characteristic attitude, on the other hand, of one who tries to follow the commandments of the Lord is admirably described by Paul: "I do not consider that I have reached the goal. All I can say is that I forget what lies behind and reach out to what lies before, and press on towards the winning post for the prize of the high calling of God in Christ Jesus." (Philippians 3:12–14)

It turns out, then, that the law of Christ works by setting up a process within us which is itself ethical activity. His precepts stir the imagination, arouse the conscience, challenge thought, and give an impetus to the will, issuing an action. In so far as we respond, holding the commandments steadily in view, reflecting upon them, and yet treating them not merely as objects for contemplation, but as spurs to action, there gradually comes to be built up in us a certain outlook on life, a bias of mind, a standard of moral judgment. The precepts cannot be directly transferred from the written page to action. They must become, through reflection and through effort, increasingly a part of our total outlook upon life, of the total bias of our minds. Then they will find expression in action appropriate to the changing situations in which we find ourselves. That is what I take to be the meaning of the "law written on the heart."

I want now to return once again to the point that the law of Christ is essentially concerned with the *quality* of the act and the *direction* in which it is moving and that this quality and this direction can be recognized at lowly levels of achievement, as well as in the highest reaches of sainthood. This has an important bearing on the question whether the law of Christ is meant only for those who are consciously committed to His allegiance—in other words, for members of the Church—or whether it has a general application to human relations at large. That includes the practical question whether, for example, at a time like this, it is the duty of the Church to call upon nations and governments to follow Christian ethical ideals, or to rebuke them for un-Christian policies.

It is often held that such lofty and difficult commands as those we have in the gospels must be addressed to those alone who have the resources of supernatural grace for their fullfilment and that it would not be reasonable to address them to anyone who does not know such resources. In consequence, the Church has, in effect, nothing to say to those who are outside its fold.

Most certainly it is true that we need the grace of God even to attempt to begin to fullfil such commands, and it is also true that nowhere but in the Church are we so exposed to the judgment and the forgiveness of God that the full obligation of these difficult commands comes home to the conscience, and courage is engendered to tackle them in a strength greater than our own.

But the question is, what do we conceive to be the meaning of the Gospel as a declaration of what God has done for man? Does it mean that when Christ came the attitude of God to men altered, or His purpose for them took a new direction, or even His character changed for

the better? Or does it mean that with the coming of Christ
there was an effective disclosure in action of what the
attitude, and purpose, and character of God always was,
always is, and always will be? To put it otherwise, is the
God of our redemption the same as the God of creation?
The inevitable answer is that He is the same God. When-
ever he confronts mankind, from the moment when
through His word man was created, God always confronts
him in the charity which was finally disclosed in Christ's
self-sacrifice. But, if this is so, then the law of the new
covenant, which is correlative with the act of God in Christ,
is aboriginal. It is the law of our creation, and its field of
application is as wide as the creation itself.

It is noteworthy that in setting forth his teaching Jesus
more than once appeals to the established order of creation
as a pointer to the law of God. One remarkable instance
is His legislation about divorce. The law of Moses, He
said, permitted divorce, but this was only a concession to
human obtuseness. "From the beginning of creation, He
created them male and female . . . and the two are to be
one flesh." Hence follows the conclusion: "Those whom
God has joined, man must not separate." (Mark 10:2-9)
That is to say, the very nature of man, as created by God,
points, if properly understood, to the law of permanent
monogamy; and now that the Kingdom of God has come,
that aboriginal law must be faced in its full implications.

Again, when He is laying down what has often been
regarded as one of the most distinctive and even the most
paradoxical elements in the Christian law, He argues from
the order of created nature: "Love your enemies, that you

may be sons of your Father in heaven; for He makes the sun shine on evil and good, and rains on just and unjust."

Once again, it is presupposed in many of His sayings that there are human relationships on the natural level, such as those of parent and child, master and servant, king and subject, friend and friend, which upon inspection disclose certain principles or maxims which are the mirror of the Creator's pattern for human life. In these maxims we may already discern something of the quality and the direction which human action must have in it if it is to conform with the ultimate law of charity. "If you, evil as you are, give good gifts to your children, how much more your Father in Heaven." In other words, parental care for children is a part of man's original endowment as a creature of God. It falls far short of the perfect fatherhood of God, but it has the same quality and moves in the same direction as the love of God Himself. Conversely, we are justified in saying, if a parent does not give his children as good gifts as he can manage, there is a breach of the law of God; and the parent is subject to this judgment, whether he is a Christian or not, because the law of God, which is revealed and interpreted in Christ, is a universal law, capable of being observed in its measure at every level, while infinite in its ultimate range.

Thus, the Church has a double duty in relation to the law of Christ. It is bound to take seriously the work of establishing a specific discipline for its own members, which shall bring the fundamental principles of the Gospel and the law of Christ to bear upon actual situations, in the world as it is. In doing this, the Church would be carrying on the work which was done by early Christian teachers in constructing the primitive *catechesis* to which I directed attention above.

But, secondly, the Church is also bound to pronounce in Christ's name moral judgments upon human conduct beyond the limits of its own membership. It does so, not in the sense that it supposes the highest Christian ideals to be directly attainable in these spheres; they are not directly attainable even within its own membership, and any attempt to suggest that they are is to diminish the moral power of the Gospel. It pronounces such judgments in the sense that unless human action, even in these spheres, has the quality and the direction demanded by the law of Christ, it is wrong and stands condemned.

It may, for instance, be neither possible nor desirable for nations to act like the man who turns the other cheek; but even at such a moment as this in the affairs of the world, human action is wrong unless it partakes of *this quality,* of patient and unself-seeking respect for the other party, however objectionable; and aims in *this direction,* towards overcoming evil with good. Unless it does so, it is not only wrong, but ultimately disastrous.

The law of Christ, we conclude, is not a specialized code of regulations for a society with optional membership. It is based upon the revelation of the nature of the eternal God, and it affirms the principles upon which His world is built and which men ignore at their peril.

We have seen that the law of Christ is "written on the heart." That remarkable expression recurs in another passage in Paul's letters, where he is making the point that the pagan world, outside the limits both of Judaism and of Christianity, is not without knowledge of God and of His law, and consequently is responsible to Him.

When pagans [he writes], who have no law, instinctively do what the law commands, then, although they have no law, they are a law to themselves, since they exhibit the effect of the law written on their hearts. Their conscience bears witness to it, and their rational processes of thought accuse or defend them, as the case may be. (Romans 2:14–15)

It appears, then, that the law of God was written on the heart of man by the very fact of his creation by God. The perversity of the human will, the depravity of human society, and all that is comprehended in the theological ideas of the fall of man and original sin may have overlaid that law, but there is something there to which the commandments of Christ can be addressed and which has the capacity of acknowledging them.

It is a part of the mission of the church to bear witness to this aboriginal law of man's creation. The count against the great anti-Christian systems which are so powerful in the world at the present time is not just that they reject *our* ethic, the ethic we happen to prefer; not that they reject the Christian ethic as one system of morals to which they prefer another system of morals. It is that they repudiate the law of man's creation. In Paul's pungent words, "They hold down the truth by their unrighteousness"—the truth, namely, about man as God's creature. Over against them, it is not for us to recommend *our* ethic, the Christian ethic as a specialized system characteristic of our community. It is for us to bear witness to what the Gospel declares about the eternal nature of God as revealed in Christ, out of which all moral obligation flows. The Christian ethic, in short, can as little make itself good in the world apart from the Gospel as the Gospel can be understood apart from its ethical implications.